L I F E W A Y S

The **Wampanoag**

R A Y M O N D   B I A L

BENCHMARK BOOKS

MARSHALL CAVENDISH
NEW YORK

SERIES CONSULTANT: JOHN BIERHORST

ACKNOWLEDGMENTS

The Wampanoag would not have been possible without the help of a number of individuals and organizations. I would like to thank the Wampanoag Tribe of Gay Head and the many helpful people in the community of Aquinnah on Martha's Vineyard who allowed me to make photographs there. I would like to especially thank Nan Doty for her gracious help and hospitality during my visit. I would like to express my deep appreciation to the tribal council for allowing me to photograph the festivities of Cranberry Day. Many fine people made my trip to Martha's Vineyard an enjoyable and memorable experience.

I would like to thank my editor Christina Gardeski for her careful review of this manuscript. I am once again indebted to John Bierhorst for his attentive reading and many helpful suggestions. As always, my deepest appreciation is for my wife Linda and my children Anna, Sarah, and Luke and for their support during the research, writing, and photography of this book.

Benchmark Books
Marshall Cavendish
99 White Plains Road
Tarrytown, New York 10591-9001
www.marshallcavendish.com
Text copyright © 2004 by Raymond Bial
Map copyright © 2004 by Marshall Cavendish Corporation
Map by Rodica Prato

Library of Congress Cataloging-in-Publication Data
Bial, Raymond.
The Wampanoag / Raymond Bial.
p. cm.—(Lifeways)
Summary: Discusses the history, culture, beliefs, changing ways,
and notable people of the Wampanoag.
Includes bibliographical references and index.
ISBN 0-7614-1683-8
1. Wampanoag Indians—History—Juvenile literature. 2. Wampanoag
Indians—Social life and customs—Juvenile literature. [1. Wampanoag
Indians. 2. Indians of North America—New England] I. Title.
II. Series: Bial, Raymond. Lifeways.
E99.W2B53 2003
974.4004'973—dc21
2003001448

Printed in Italy
6 5 4 3 2 1

Photo Research by Anne Burns Images

Cover Photos by Raymond Bial

The photographs in this book are used with permission and through the courtesy of: *Granger Collection*: pp. 1, 16, 80, 110. *Raymond Bial*: pp. 6, 8, 9, 11, 13, 19, 22, 24, 25, 27, 30, 34, 35, 45, 46, 49, 50, 57, 60, 62, 64, 65, 66, 67, 70, 72, 73, 74, 75, 77, 90, 91, 93, 94, 95, 97, 98, 100, 101. *National Museum of the American Indian, Smithsonian Institution*: pp. 32 (N2785), 37 (N06535), 39 (N20349), 40 (N20345), 55 (N20342), 59 (N20256), 74 & 75 (N15814), 82 & 83 (N15755). © *Archive Photos*: p. 43.

This book is dedicated to the Wampanoag who have long made their home in southern New England.

Contents

Author's Note

At the dawn of the twentieth century, Native Americans were thought to be a vanishing race. However, despite four hundred years of warfare, deprivation, and disease, American Indians have not gone away. Countless thousands have lost their lives, but over the course of the twentieth century the populations of native tribes grew tremendously. Even as American Indians struggle to adapt to modern Western life, they have also kept the flame of their traditions alive—the language, religion, stories, and the everyday ways of life. An exhilarating renaissance in Native American culture is now sweeping the nation from coast to coast.

The Lifeways books depict the social and cultural life of the major nations, from the early history of native peoples in North America to their present-day struggles for survival and dignity. Historical and contemporary photographs of traditional subjects, as well as period illustrations, are blended throughout each book so that readers may gain a sense of family life in a tipi, a hogan, or a longhouse.

No single book can comprehensively portray the intricate and varied lifeways of an entire tribe, or nation. I only hope that young people will come away with a deeper appreciation for the rich tapestry of Indian culture—both then and now—and a keen desire to learn more about these first Americans.

1. Origins

For many generations, the Wampanoag have lived on or near the coast of the Atlantic Ocean, including what is now Martha's Vineyard.

FOR COUNTLESS GENERATIONS, THE WAMPANOAG (WAM-PUH-NO-UG) made their home in what are now the states of Massachusetts and Rhode Island. Living in small villages, they passed down their history and traditions through storytelling. In the evenings, the young and old gathered around the fire to listen to the elders recount the tribe's origins. These stories allowed people to gain a better understanding of their place in the universe. Many of the stories of the Wampanoag of Aquinnah on Martha's Vineyard center on a benevolent giant named Moshup. Helen Manning, a Wampanoag elder born on Martha's Vineyard, recalls her grandmother telling her that Moshup was "taller than the tallest tree and as large around as the spread of a full-grown pine." Here is a story about how Moshup created the island of Noepe.

Moshup Shapes the Island Noepe

Many years ago, Noepe, or Martha's Vineyard, was not an island. It was part of the seventy-mile Cape Cod peninsula that curves gracefully into the Atlantic Ocean. When Moshup was a boy, he accompanied his father on hunting and fishing trips along the coast. Both father and son towered over the tallest trees. From that height, they could gaze over all the lands of the Wampanoag in Massachusetts and Rhode Island. Moshup glanced over the coastal plain and told his father that he was magically drawn to Noepe and wished to settle there.

Moshup was not happy on the mainland. However, everything appeared to be perfect at Noepe, except that no one lived there. One day Moshup called his many cousins together. He told them of the beauty of Noepe and the abundance of fish in the seas and game in the forests. Moshup decided to make a new home on Noepe and he invited his cousins to accompany him.

Once on Noepe, Moshup and his cousins wandered through the shadowy forest. They waded across bogs and marshes and trudged over sand dunes. Weary from his long journey, Moshup began to drag his heavy feet, leaving a track into which a little water trickled. It was just a silver thread, but the ocean winds, the rolling waves, and the tides quickly deepened and widened the channel. In rushed the waters of the sea to separate Noepe from the mainland.

According to traditional stories, the ocean winds and waves separated the island of Noepe, or Martha's Vineyard, from the mainland.

Moshup's cousins and their families settled at various places on the island. They established small villages, each of which was governed by a sachem and a council of elders. Known as sachemships, these settlements included Taakemmy, or mid-island place to grind corn; Nunne-peg, or the water people; and Chappaquiddick, or separate island. Pleased that his cousins had established a peaceful and prosperous society, Moshup founded his own sachemship at Aquinnah Cliffs. He lived there with his wife Squant and their many children in a place known as Moshup's Den. He taught his cousins how to catch fish, clams, and sea mammals and, over the ages, helped them to prosper in many other ways. To this day, in the spirit of Moshup, the Wampanoag care for the island of Martha's Vineyard.

Early History

In the early seventeenth century between 6,500 and 12,000 Wampanoag lived in what is now eastern Rhode Island, the coastal areas of southeastern Massachusetts, and several offshore islands. The Wampanoag included the Nauset of Cape Cod and the Sakonnet of southeastern Rhode Island. Various tribes of the islands, including Martha's Vineyard, the Elizabeth Islands, and Nantucket, were also counted among the Wampanoag. At the time, their grand sachem, or principal leader, was Massasoit. Originally the Wampanoag were known as the Pokanoket, after the name of Massasoit's home village, which was located at or near the present-day town of Warren, Rhode Island. The name *Wampanoag* is probably derived from *Wapanacki*, which means "people of the east" or "people of the dawn."

After helping his cousins establish villages on Noepe, Moshup made a home for his family at Aquinnah Cliffs.

People have inhabited the region from twelve to fifteen thousand years. As early as 2270 B.C., people were hunting and fishing on Martha's Vineyard. People were settling on the island by A.D. 1380. Over time, the Wampanoag adapted to living in the woods and on the water and learned to provide for themselves. The men built circular houses, stalked deer, traded for various goods, and fought with neighboring peoples. Women managed their households, took care of children, planted crops, gathered wild berries, caught shellfish, and made clothing, mats, and baskets. For many generations, they prospered in this territory of forests, marshes, and coastal waters. Then, in the early 1500s, the native people in New England encountered European explorers and traders. At the first contact with Europeans, it is estimated that there may have been as many as twelve thousand Wampanoag people. The first documented encounters occurred with the Mashpee Wampanoag of Cape Cod in the first decade of the seventeenth century. Martin Pring, Bartholomew Gosnold, and Samuel de Champlain met the Wampanoag as they explored the coastline of Cape Cod. By 1620, when the English began to establish colonies in the region, diseases carried by the early European seafarers had already devastated the native populations in New England. The Wampanoag were so weakened by these diseases that they were more vulnerable to raids from the more northerly tribes, especially the Eastern Abenaki of Maine. Moreover, they were being pressed by the Narragansett of western Rhode Island, who had expanded eastward into Wampanoag territory after the disastrous epidemics of 1616–1619. Wampanoag towns such as Patuxet (Plymouth) were annihilated by illness and conflict. Harried by other tribes, the Wampanoag allied themselves with the struggling, but well-armed Pilgrims. Fifty years of peace followed. More than a century later, President Abraham Lincoln proclaimed a national Thanksgiving holiday in 1863. However, for the Wampanoag, it was hardly a season to express gratitude. They mourned a great tragedy—the loss of their lands and loved ones—and the desperate struggle by those people who survived.

Thanksgiving

In the autumn of 1621, the Pilgrims invited Grand Sachem Massasoit and the Wampanoag people to join them in a feast now remembered as "the first Thanksgiving." However, only many years later, in the nineteenth century, did this gathering come to be associated with the American holiday. The Thanksgiving of today more likely dates to a traditional English harvest festival that the Pilgrims celebrated in their new homeland. The feast evolved into a yearly autumn celebration in New England. In 1777, the Continental Congress recommended that the colonies set aside a day of Thanksgiving. In 1863, President Abraham Lincoln that year called for two days of Thanksgiving—one to be observed on August 6 to express gratitude for the Union victory at Gettysburg, and the other on the last Thursday in November to give thanks for the nation's bounty.

For many Wampanoag, the First Thanksgiving at Plymouth, Massachusetts, symbolizes loss—of their land and their cherished way of life.

Through the nineteenth century, the traditions of the holiday emphasized turkeys and family reunions, not Pilgrims and Native Americans. It was not until after the turn of the twentieth century that the pleasant image of colonists and natives sharing a feast came to be admired. By World War I, popular art in schoolbooks, literature, and postcards firmly established the images of Pilgrims and

New England natives celebrating the first Thanksgiving—Pilgrims somberly clothed in black and feathered natives feasting on turkey, cranberries, pumpkins, and squash.

No Wampanoag accounts of the feast have been found. The only English written records come from William Bradford, governor of Plymouth Colony, and Edward Winslow, who took part in the first Thanksgiving. Bradford apparently proclaimed the celebration but does not mention the holiday in *History of Plimoth Plantation*, his history of the colony. Winslow does mention the thanksgiving feast in a letter to a friend in England dated December 11, 1621:

"Our harvest being gotten in, our governor sent four men on fowling, that so we might after a more special manner rejoice together, after we had gathered the fruit of our labors. . . . [For nearly a week] amongst other recreations, we exercised our arms, many of the Indians coming amongst us, and amongst the rest their greatest king Massasoit, with some ninety men, whom for three days we entertained and feasted, and they went out and killed five deer, which they brought to the plantation and bestowed on our governor, and upon the captain, and others."

Whatever its history, Thanksgiving—for most Americans—emphasizes the significant ideas of sharing and harmony. Yet, in view of the long record of broken promises, many native leaders would agree with Russell Peters, who, as president of the Mashpee Wampanoag Indian Tribal Council, said, "For Indians, Thanksgiving is now a day of fasting and mourning."

The People and the Land

The Wampanoag lived in scattered, allied villages in what is now eastern Rhode Island and southeastern Massachusetts. Their homeland surrounded Narragansett Bay and included all of Cape Cod, Martha's Vineyard, and Nantucket. Dotted with islands, the jagged coastline had many coves, inlets, and bays. Shimmering beaches, shifting dunes, saltwater marshes, and fields of seaside goldenrod lined the coastal lowlands. Cranberry bogs gave way to stands of scrub oaks, gradually rising terrain, and steep, forested hills. Cape Cod, a sandy, curved peninsula, tapered into the blue waters of the Atlantic Ocean. South of Cape Cod and amid several small islands were Martha's Vineyard and Nantucket Island.

The region was a blend of forests, rivers, lakes, marshes, and coastal waters. It was a rocky landscape once scoured by glaciers, yet temperate enough that people could grow corn, beans, and squash in clearings around their villages or along the coast. Winters could be brutally cold, with heavy snowfalls, yet the summer growing season was relatively long. The soil was not particularly fertile, but generations of oak, hickory, chestnut, and maple leaves had decayed on the forest floor creating a layer of rich humus that covered the bedrock.

Amid the wilderness, there were extensive patches of cleared, settled land. In these clearings were wigwams and fields of crops. Every spring and fall, the Wampanoag set fire to the underbrush in the forests around their villages. The ashes helped to fertilize

*W*ampanoag territory included open land near the beaches and clearings in the forest, where people gathered berries or planted crops.

the soil. Towering trees remained in an open forest and sunlight penetrated to the ground, encouraging the growth of new plants. This careful burning improved hunting and gathering. Deer could forage on the tender, young shoots, and game had less cover. Hunters could move easily through the forest, and women could gather the wild blueberries that flourished on the burned areas.

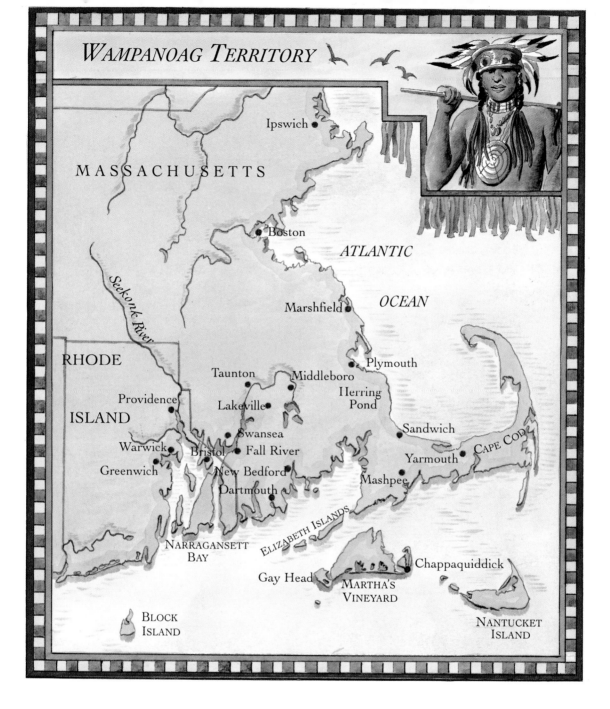

WAMPANOAG TERRITORY

Ipswich

MASSACHUSETTS

Boston

ATLANTIC

Marshfield

OCEAN

Seekonk River

RHODE

Plymouth

Taunton   Middleboro

Herring
Pond

Providence   Lakeville

ISLAND   Sandwich

Swansea   CAPE COD

Warwick   Bristol   Fall River   Yarmouth

Greenwich   New Bedford   Mashpee

Dartmouth

NARRAGANSETT
BAY   ELIZABETH ISLANDS

Chappaquiddick

Gay Head   MARTHA'S
VINEYARD

BLOCK
ISLAND   NANTUCKET
ISLAND

This map shows the historic territory of the Wampanoag when they first encountered European colonists in the early 1600s.

For generations the Wampanoag routinely managed the woods, making seasonal rounds to hunt, fish, gather, and trade with other peoples. They hunted large game, especially deer and moose. They stalked black bears for their meat and fat and thick coats. Other animals, including raccoon, opossum, woodchucks, otter, cottontail rabbits, gray and red squirrels, foxes, and even wolves, were caught for their meat and fur. The Wampanoag also hunted birds, especially wild turkeys, grouse, and passenger pigeons, along with ducks, geese, and other migrating waterfowl. In the clear streams and lakes, they caught fish with spears, nets, and hooks and lines. To trap eels and fish swimming upriver to spawn they built weirs of stones interlaced with branches. These migrating fish included suckers, sturgeon, shad, pickerel, and walleyed pike.

Over time, the Wampanoag shifted their seasonal migrations to partake of the bounty of fish and shellfish in the coastal waters. Once a year, they moved to the ocean to dig oysters and quahogs in the shallow water and to catch saltwater fish, such as alewives or the occasional swordfish. They also trapped lobsters and crabs for their succulent meat. It is likely that the Wampanoag also snatched seabirds from their nests and caught sea mammals, including seals, porpoises, and whales.

Their location in New England adversely affected the Wampanoag when European fishermen, traders, and colonists landed on their shores. Tribes living in the interior were not immediately endangered by the arrival of these newcomers. However, the Wampanoag living on or near the coast had to directly contend with the Europeans and were

To this day, the Wampanoag continue to look upon the land and water as their home, as well as the home of their ancestors.

the first to be exposed to the diseases they introduced. Native people had little or no resistance to these illnesses, and soon their numbers were so reduced that they could not keep their land. In the early 1600s, epidemics swept through the region and devastated the Wampanoag. The Pilgrims were left with their pick of abandoned villages and cultivated fields. One newcomer commented, "Thousands of men have lived there, which died in a great plague now long since; and pity it was and is to see so many goodly fields, and so well seated, without men to dress and manure the same."

Today, many descendants of the Wampanoag continue to make their home in the region of their ancestors.

2. Villages

*Most of the territory of the Wampanoag was
laced with broad rivers and streams,
which seasonally provided
an abundance of fish.*

THE WAMPANOAG LIVED IN VILLAGES. THE PEOPLE IN EACH VILLAGE made use of a particular region. During the winter, people lived in the main village, usually located in deep woods along a stream or lake. When spring came, families took down their houses and moved separately or in small groups to outlying areas where food could be hunted, gathered, or cultivated.

During the spring fish runs when thousands of spawning fish were swimming upstream, people left the main village and moved to camps near the rivers. People from several villages often camped on the banks, where they visited, played games, and enjoyed celebrations. In the summer, families dispersed into camps of one or more houses strung along the coast. They tended patches of corn and other crops near their summer camps and took short trips to pick fruits and berries and to catch lobsters. After the harvest in the early fall, people moved again, back to the main village. Even during the late autumn, families were often away at hunting camps. However, as the snows deepened, these families returned to the village to settle around their fires during the long, cold winter.

After the English established colonies in their territory, the Wampanoag often sought refuge in hilltop villages surrounded by a high wall known as a palisade. A palisade was made of sharpened poles stuck vertically into the ground and lashed together.

In the early seventeenth century, there were at least thirty Wampanoag villages. The villages were composed of circular lodges known as wigwams and rectangular dwellings known as longhouses.

Many people once lived along the Atlantic Coast where they caught fish and gathered shellfish on the sandy beaches.

The family's cornfields were usually situated near their dwelling. Every village had a central open space for meetings and ceremonies, as well as a sweat lodge.

Wampanoag Houses

Dwellings known as *weetos* varied in size and shape. Smaller, dome-shaped wigwams were round at the base and about fifteen feet in diameter. Larger, oblong or oval longhouses were about thirty feet wide and fifty to one hundred feet long. These houses were large enough to shelter from forty to fifty people. Several families shared the larger dwellings when they came together in a winter village. When they were ocean fishing or gardening during the other seasons, they took shelter in smaller weetos occupied by one or two families.

Both wigwams and longhouses were made of pole frames covered with woven mats or wide sheets of bark. Bark-covered lodges were warmer than mat-sheathed lodges. Winter dwellings were usually covered with bark, while the more portable houses in the seasonal camps were covered with mats. Wigwams were often set up over a shallow pit lined with cattails, pine needles, or other insulating materials. There were no windows. The only light came from a low doorway, often covered with a mat or sheet of bark, and a smokehole in the roof, which could also be covered in rainy weather. A fire was built in a shallow hole in the center of the earthen floor. A longhouse had an entrance at each end and a row of smokeholes along the roof. Each family had its own fire and there was a row of fire pits for cooking meals and providing warmth in the winter.

Bulrush mats, often decorated with paintings, lined the interior walls. Mats were also used as bedding on the floor of the wigwam. In a longhouse, mats for bedding were arranged on raised platforms along the walls. About a foot and a half above the floor, these platforms were made of forked posts stuck in the ground to support horizontal poles. Furs served as blankets. A large bed accommodated an entire family and any visitors. Inside the dwelling, there were bundles of rushes, hemp, and other materials for making mats and baskets, along with tools and weapons.

Other furnishings included baskets, bags, clay pots, birch-bark boxes, and containers for food storage and preparation. People ate meals with carved wooden bowls, plates, and spoons. Pots were hung over the fire from a square frame made of forked branches supporting slender poles. Cooking pots were originally clay, but the Wampanoag later traded with Europeans for durable iron, brass, or copper kettles. There was always a pot of simmering food or a hunk of meat slowly roasting over the fire, so that people could eat whenever they were hungry. During damp weather, fish and meat were dried on wooden racks placed near the fire.

Chiefs had larger, more elaborately furnished homes than did the other villagers. Poor people had to take shelter in small huts. The Wampanoag also built large dance houses that could be one or two hundred feet long. Other village structures included watch houses in the cornfields, where people shooed away hungry birds, and menstrual huts, where women retired for a few days every month.

Sweat lodges were also part of the village. Individuals purified themselves in these buildings. Sweat lodges were made by excavating a small cave in a hillside over which a wooden structure was erected and covered with mats. This formed an interior about eight feet in diameter and four feet high. Rocks were heated over a fire until the sweat lodge became very hot. The sweat lodge was located near a stream or lake so that people could run out and plunge into the cold water.

Nearly fifty years after the landing of the Pilgrims, most Wampanoag were still living in *weetos*. But they gradually adopted European-style frame houses with shingled roofs.

The Wampanoag built dome-shaped homes and other structures, like this sweat lodge, which they covered with mats.

Family, Clan, and Community

Wampanoag society had three basic social classes: the sachem and the members of his family; the other members of the community; and the war captives who lived as servants. Within the first and second of these categories, there were great differences in wealth and social position. The wealthy and noble people had the finest mats in their houses. They had striking tattoos on their faces and wore considerable wampum on their bodies. Men of these classes often had more than one wife and servants.

A sachem governed a certain territory. Sub-sachems were responsible for smaller areas and villages within that territory. A sachem inherited his position through the male line, that is, a son succeeded his father upon his death. Occasionally, the wife of a sachem assumed the position when he died. Daughters and nephews could also become sachems, if the leader's son was too young. The position was then held for the son until he came of age. The sachem oversaw the allotment of land and collected tribute from his followers. A sachem with more followers enjoyed greater wealth, so a leader tried to please his people. Otherwise they might leave and join another sachem. A sub-sachem attended to the personal needs of his group, such as resolving disputes.

Although a sachem was supposed to have absolute power, on important matters he was advised by a tribal council of village and clan chiefs, known as *pnieses*. The village and clan chiefs also served as war leaders and personal guards for the sachem when he traveled. The sachem also consulted respected elders and shamans, called *powwows*.

Wampanoag communities were centered on strong families, which included grandparents, and membership in various clans.

Villages were independent of each other, but sometimes formed alliances. After the epidemics of 1616–1619, the Wampanoag became more unified as a people.

Wampanoag society was also organized by family and clan. Like many other native people of eastern North America, families were matrilineal, meaning that people traced their ancestry through the mother's side. The Wampanoag were further organized into a number of clans whose members traced their descent from a common ancestor.

3. Lifeways

The beaches of Wampanoag territory
are still marked with footpaths
that once led to villages and
places for hunting, fishing,
and gathering.

Cycle of Life

The Wampanoag followed a seasonal cycle of hunting, fishing, gathering, planting, and harvesting. They noted the passage of time by observing the celestial bodies and the four seasons. The time of day was measured by the height of the sun, the months were determined by the phases of the moon, and the seasons were marked by the changing weather. Similarly, people followed the cycle of life, from birth to death.

Birth. A woman continued to work in the fields and village until she was about to give birth. She then retired to a lodge where, with the help of one or more older women serving as midwives, she had her baby. If she had problems in the delivery, a powwow was asked to call upon powerful spirits for assistance.

The newborn was coated with grease and clothed in a beaver skin or other soft fur, then wrapped onto a cradleboard. For most of the day, the baby remained safely on the cradleboard, always close to its mother. The mother carried the baby on her back as she worked outside. She leaned the cradleboard against the inside wall of the lodge, where the infant could watch her as she cooked meals.

The mother often sang soothing lullabies to her baby. Usually quiet and content, babies seldom cried. The mother nursed her baby for at least a year, after which she began to give the child small morsels of food.

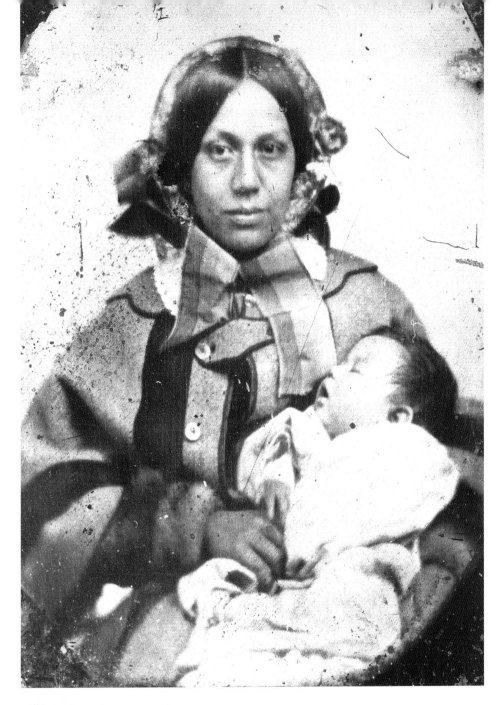

For countless generations, Wampanoag mothers have lovingly cared for their newborn babies.

Childhood. The Wampanoag were very fond of their children. Children were rarely disciplined but instead were taught through a positive example. One English colonist thought that the children were "sawcie, bold, and undutifull." However, the Wampanoag wished their children to be not only respectful, but also spirited and independent.

Children learned by watching and imitating their parents and other adults as they worked at various chores. Boys shot small bows and arrows to practice skills they would need in hunting and warfare. Girls played with small cooking pots and helped plant and tend crops from an early age.

Children enjoyed playing many kinds of games. They also learned about the beliefs and traditions of the Wampanoag by listening to stories told by their parents and grandparents.

Coming-of-Age. As children approached adulthood, they underwent initiation ceremonies. There were ceremonies for girls, but little is known about them today. A boy at puberty was blindfolded and taken into the wilderness during the fall. He was left there with a bow and arrows, hatchet, and knife. He had to provide for himself through the winter, when game was scarce. Toward spring, the men of the village went to find the young man and take him home. Afterward, he was sent out every morning with a knowledgeable man to gather herbs and roots. He learned to make a bitter and poisonous tea from the plant juices, along with an antidote. Once he was able to withstand a dose of this tea, the men and women sang and danced. The young man was then considered an adult.

Although their styles of dress changed as they adopted new ways of life, the Wampanoag continued to cherish their children.

As they came of age, Wampanoag women prepared to be married and raise families of their own.

At the time of initiation, both girls and boys received their new adult names. They were then ready for marriage.

Marriage. When a man wanted to marry, he first spoke with the woman and then with her parents. The village leader also had to approve of the marriage. The man gave the bride's parents wampum or other goods as payment for the loss of their daughter. The man's parents and other relatives might help him by contributing some of these gifts.

Prominent families built alliances through political marriages between sachems and women of high standing from other villages. Sachems often had two or more wives. Anyone wealthy enough to support several wives was highly esteemed. Most men had one wife.

If a woman's husband mistreated her, she could leave him. A husband could banish an unfaithful wife. However, people seldom lived alone. Widows, widowers, and divorced individuals usually moved in with their relatives until they married again.

Death. The dead were placed in a sitting position in a grave lined with mats. Weapons, tools, wampum, ornaments, and other belongings needed in the afterlife were buried with the body. The grave was located in or near the house of the deceased. The sheathing was removed from the weeto, leaving only the frame, and was then abandoned.

Painting their faces black, men and women mourned the loss of their loved ones. Gathering around the grave, family and friends cried in grief and mourned for many days. When a sachem or other prominent individual died, people mourned for a year.

It was believed that the souls of good people upon their death journeyed to the southwest where they would live as they had in the physical world. During this journey to the spirit world, the deceased faced many hazards, including a vicious dog. The souls of the less fortunate were condemned to wander, lost and restless, in the world. People believed that these restless, unhappy ghosts lingered near camps and villages, inflicting misfortune and illness on the living. However, once they reached the afterlife, the souls of good, contented people enjoyed an idyllic life.

Warfare

The Wampanoag traditionally allied with the Massachusett. Wampanoag enemies included the Eastern Abenaki and the Narragansett, and later the English colonists. Before going to war, men painted their faces—either all black, black and white, black and red, or spotted with a variety of colors—to make themselves appear fearsome to their enemies. They fought with wooden bows and arrows tipped with stone, bone, eagle claw, or crab-tail points. Wielding ball-headed war clubs, they protected themselves with bark shields. Leaders often carried long spears. Warriors used sharp knives to take scalps.

It is believed that the pnieses formed a prestigious military society. Members of this society provided leadership in battle. Boys who showed promise of great strength and good character—especially

*W*hen they matured, young men became warriors who defended their people and their land.

courage, honesty, and judgment—were selected to become pnieses. These young men endured rigorous training. When deemed ready, they were initiated into the society in a ceremony in which they underwent daunting physical and spiritual ordeals. Bold and courageous, pnieses considered themselves impervious to the weapons of their enemies.

The Wampanoag went to war for many reasons, including to avenge a murder and to settle disputes over territory and power struggles among leaders. The sachem or a group within the community could call for a war. The sachem and his council then met and decided whether to undertake the war. Once it was decided to go to war, the warriors danced and listened to speeches and readied themselves for battle. As the warriors approached the enemy camp, they slipped from one tree to another. Whenever possible, they tried to make a surprise attack when their opponents were sleeping or taking shelter during a storm. After the attack, the warriors just as quickly retreated with their plunder and prisoners. Captives were often tortured and killed. Some, especially women and children, were adopted into the tribe. When they returned to their village, the warriors celebrated their victory.

Hunting and Fishing

The coastal region of southern New England abounded in wildlife, both in the water and on the land. In the spring, people gathered at the falls of rivers to catch herring and other fish migrating upstream in spawning runs. They used spears, nets,

The Wampanoag often turned to the sea as a plentiful source of food, including many kinds of shellfish.

and lines fitted with bone hooks. Sometimes, they built weirs across the streams. They also caught freshwater fish, such as trout, perch, pike, catfish, and occasionally large sturgeon. People remained in the fishing camps until planting time, when they moved to the coast to tend small fields. There, through the summer and into the fall, they caught saltwater fish, including bass, cod, and haddock. After moving inland for the winter, they occasionally caught fish through holes in the ice on ponds and

When they moved to the coast during the summer and autumn, the
Wampanoag cultivated small fields and caught saltwater fish.

lakes. However, in Rhode Island, the Wampanoag continued to fish in the ocean through the cold months. Fish were eaten fresh or dried and then stored for use in the lean months of winter.

During the spring migration, men hunted ducks, Canada geese, and swans. Hunters netted turkeys, ruffed grouse, pigeons, and cranes or shot them with bows and arrows. At night they snatched cormorants from their roosts on the offshore rocks. They also caught turtles for their delicious meat. People sometimes butchered whales stranded on the beach. In warm weather, they caught seals, valued for their meat and oil, while the animals slept on the rocks. Women trapped lobsters, whose meat was used for fish bait or dried and smoked for winter use. They also gathered shellfish, such as oysters, clams, and scallops, which they cooked over heated rocks or dried and stored for the winter.

Men hunted game, ranging in size from gray squirrels to black bears. Otters, muskrats, beavers, raccoons, fox, and wolves and an occasional moose, were also hunted or trapped. However, they mostly hunted white-tailed deer, the animal that supplied most of the meat in the diet. Men stalked deer, and caught them in traps and snares throughout the year, but they especially hunted these fleet-footed animals in the fall and early winter. Men, women, and children sometimes joined in large, communal hunts in which they drove a large number of deer into a V-shaped fence, a mile or two long and made of brush and branches. The deer were chased through the wide opening and toward the narrow end where hunters had set traps or shot the confined animals.

When the snow began to sweep over the land, people moved back to their main villages in the woods and valleys where they were shielded from the cold winds. From December or January until April, they settled in these winter villages. They occasionally trapped game but lived mostly on their stores of food.

Gathering and Gardening

In early spring, the Wampanoag tapped maple trees for sap that they cooked down to make sweet syrup. Through the spring, summer, and fall, women gathered roots, berries, fruits, and nuts. Roots were stored as winter food while wild strawberries, blackberries, raspberries, blueberries, and grapes were eaten fresh. Currants and other berries were dried and stored for later use. In the autumn, women collected acorns, walnuts, and chestnuts, all of which were shelled, dried, and stored for use when food was scarce. These nuts were pounded into flour and added to soups and stews. Acorns had to be thoroughly boiled to remove the bitter taste. Cranberries were picked in the low-lying ground on Martha's Vineyard and in southern New England. Hemp was gathered to make nets, fishing lines, ropes, and twined baskets.

The Wampanoag raised corn, beans, pumpkins, and squash. Corn became their most important crop. The kernels had a variety of colors, including red, blue, yellow, and white.

The first European visitors were impressed by the number of well-tended fields along the shores and villages. To clear land for a new field, men chopped down trees with stone axes, leaving stumps about

Through the spring, summer, and autumn, the Wampanoag spent much of their time gathering foods, such as these black raspberries.

three feet above the ground. They burned the trunks and branches, and then the women planted seeds among the stumps. Over time, as the stumps rotted, they were rooted out and lugged from the fields. In preparation for planting, women loosened the soil with clamshell hoes. Then they made small hills about three feet apart using horseshoe crab shells. In each hill, they placed three or four kernels of corn and the same number of beans. They often buried small fish

Wild blueberries were among the different kinds of fruits and berries gathered by the Wampanoag.

in the hills as fertilizer. Throughout the growing season, they diligently cultivated the fields with hoes. After several years, a field was sometimes allowed to lie fallow, or unplanted, to recover its fertility. Then the brush was burned away and the field was planted again. Women usually did all of the planting, cultivating, and harvesting, although children and old men sometimes helped. The only crop grown by the men was tobacco for use in rituals.

As the corn ripened, watch houses were built in the fields where women or older children chased away the hungry birds. Sometimes, hawks were caught, tamed, and kept near the fields to scare the other birds away. Some corn was picked and eaten fresh like sweet corn, but most of the crop was allowed to fully ripen and the kernels to become hard. In the autumn, this hard corn and the other crops were harvested. Some of the harvest was eaten fresh but most of it was dried for later use. Women placed the dried corn, beans, and squash in woven sacks or baskets and stored them in caches, or underground pits, lined with mats. The pits were covered with mats and sometimes planks. These provisions were used as needed during the fall and winter. The first Pilgrims on Cape Cod sometimes found these caches and raided them.

Meat and fish were usually boiled or roasted on a forked stick. Small pieces of dried or fresh meat, fish, and shellfish were added to soups and stews. Clam juice was used as a seasoning in place of salt. Ears of fresh corn were boiled, while kernels of hard corn were parched, or dried, over hot coals and ground into a coarse meal. This cornmeal was added to stews or cooked into a thick porridge. Cornmeal was also made into a dough flavored with crushed strawberries, then shaped into loaves, wrapped in leaves, and baked in ashes to make bread. Cornmeal and powdered dried currants were boiled and made into cakes, which the Wampanoag favored.

Following is a modern recipe for a dessert that is very popular with the Wampanoag.

Cranberry Crisp

Cranberries are a delicious ingredient in many dishes, including desserts. Here is a tasty recipe, compliments of Aquinnah tribal elder Helen Manning, that is a favorite at the Fall Social on Cranberry Day.

Ingredients

4 cups whole fresh cranberries
2 cups brown sugar
2 cups flour
1 cup uncooked oatmeal
1 stick butter, cut into pieces
pinch of cinnamon

Directions

Mix together the cranberries, one cup brown sugar, one cup flour, and cinnamon. Place this mixture in a well-greased baking pan or dish. Mix one cup brown sugar, one cup flour, the oatmeal, and stick of butter. Spread this mixture over the cranberries and bake at 375 degrees until the top is brown and the fruit bubbles—about thirty-five minutes.

Clothing and Jewelry

"Wampum, made of quahog shell, is as precious and dignitary as any gem to the Wampanoag. It sustains our health, critiques our history, and adorns our apparel."

—Joan Avant Tavares, Mashpee Wampanoag

Women made all the clothing for their families from animal skins. Deer, which were abundant in the woods and fields, provided the most popular materials. Deerskins were tough, yet thin enough to be made pliable by tanning into buckskin. Deerskins were also large enough so that clothing could be made without sewing many pieces together. Moose skins were sometimes used to make clothing, but these heavy hides were better suited for moccasins.

Deer hides were first scraped to remove the hair and flesh. Then the rawhide was tanned into buckskin by laboriously working oils into the material until it became soft. The buckskin was then smoked over a fire to give it a tan color. If buckskin leggings, shirts, and dresses got wet, they could be wrung out and hung by the fire to dry without becoming stiff. If a deer was killed in winter the thick coat of hair was usually left on. These hides were used for cloaks and bedding.

Women wore wraparound skirts tied with a belt, and blouses that hung from the shoulders. They also wore moccasins. After European contact, they wore dresses made of two deerskins sewn together and with straps at the shoulders. Men wore buckskin breechcloths and moccasins. Buckskin clothing was often decorated with quillwork. During the summer, everyone went barefoot but carried moccasins in case they had to travel over rough ground. Both men and women wore buckskin leggings when traveling through scratchy undergrowth. Leggings were also worn, especially by old people, during cold weather.

Men and women often wore animal skin capes, drawn under the right arm and over the left shoulder. When traveling, the robe was tightly cinched with a belt. The bare shoulder was covered by another piece in cold weather. Women's capes were nearly twice as long as those for men. During the summer, they wore deerskin capes sewn with the fur side out. Winter robes were made of deer, beaver, otter, raccoon, bear, and fox skins sewn together with the fur inside. They also made cloaks of woven turkey feathers, hemp, or grass.

Men and women liked to wear jewelry. They adorned themselves with shell and bone necklaces and brass or copper earrings. Men wore breastplates and bandoliers made of flat, hammered brass or copper. Bandoliers were a type of belt drawn diagonally over the chest and shoulder or around the waist. Breastplates were sometimes made of rows of copper tubes about four inches long and a quarter inch in diameter. Shorter copper tubes were strung together for head-bands and necklaces.

The Wampanoag smeared their skin with animal grease or vegetable oil as protection against insects and the cold. Both men and women carefully combed and oiled their hair every day. Generally, they wore their hair long, and it was believed that wearing a ponytail made it grow faster. Women often cut their hair when they got married and wore a head covering until the hair grew back. Young

*I*n later days the Wampanoag adopted a transitional manner of dress that recalled their own tribal past, as well as more widespread Native American styles.

men who were not yet warriors usually had short hair. People sometimes cut bangs in the front and wore the rest of their hair either loose or braided. Some men may have pulled out all of their hair except for a scalp lock. They adorned their hair with turkey or eagle feathers, fox tails, strips of hide dyed red, and other ornaments.

By the early 1600s, wampum had become the most popular type of shell beads used in ornaments. Wampum was most often fashioned from the quahog, or hard-shelled clam. Tubular beads were cut from whole shells. A hole was then made in each bead with a stone drill. After Europeans introduced metal tools, the holes were made with metal drills. Belts of these small purple and white shell beads were also used as a kind of money. People wore bracelets, necklaces, headbands, and belts made of wampum. Collars, caps, and ear pendants were also made of wampum.

The Wampanoag also adorned themselves with tattoos and body paint. To create a tattoo, a sharp instrument was used to lift and pierce the skin and a black pigment was rubbed into the wound. Figures of animals, such as bears, deer, moose, wolves, eagles, or hawks, were applied, most often on the cheeks. People also branded geometric shapes on the arms and chest with a hot iron.

Before painting their bodies, the Wampanoag greased themselves to provide a bond for the dry pigment. Then they applied a dry pigment of red, yellow, white, or black powder to their skins. Red pigment was most often used in the hair. The face was painted with multiple colors or a single color. During times of mourning, people painted their faces black with soot and ashes. Warriors painted themselves when they were about to go into battle. Both men and women painted their faces for ceremonies and games.

Handicrafts

The Wampanoag crafted many of the tools, weapons, and household objects needed in their daily life from wood. Men shaped wood into bows and arrow shafts, while women made hoes with wooden handles and clamshell blades. The inner bark, or bast, from trees was woven into baskets and other goods. From pine bark, they obtained red dye, turpentine, and pitch. Some artisans were especially skilled at carving wooden bowls and spoons from burls, which had the advantage of not being easily split along the grain.

The Wampanoag wove baskets and carved wooden bowls that were both beautiful and useful.

People used birch bark to make a variety of objects, including boxes and canoes. To make a swift, graceful canoe, sheets of birch bark were sewn over a wood frame and the seams were sealed with pine pitch. Most often, however, men labored long hours to make dugout canoes. Some were as long as fifty feet and large enough to hold forty people, although most carried about ten to fifteen people. The men first chopped down a tree with a stone ax. Then, over the course of ten to twelve days, they hollowed out the trunk with small, controlled fires. They smoothed the inside with shell scrapers and shaped the outside with stone hatchets. Finally, they sanded the entire craft with a rough stone.

Women used buckskin not only for making clothes, but also for fashioning pouches for carrying tobacco and personal objects and for storing food. They also made a variety of everyday objects from various plant materials, such as bulrushes, bent grass, corn husks, hemp, and flag leaves. Women wove bulrushes or flag leaves into mats and sewed the mats together with hemp thread and a bone needle. Mats served as sheathing for houses and as lining for the floor. Fine mats were used for sitting. Food was spread out on fine mats to dry.

The Wampanoag were skilled in making soft and smooth, yet strong cords. Cord was usually made from hemp. Long fibers from the stem were braided until they had attained the desired length and thickness of thread, string, or rope. The thread was used in weaving baskets, sewing together mats, and making capes of twisted turkey feathers. People used cords of twisted fibers to

*W*ampanoag men have long been renowned as skillful, knowledgeable, and courageous fishermen in the waters of the Atlantic Ocean.

Expert weavers, the Wampanoag made cords, fishnets, baskets, and other objects that were essential in their everyday life.

lash together the framework of their weetos. Hemp strings were used as fishing lines or looped into fishnets. Cords were woven into large bags for storing food.

Women wove baskets in many sizes and shapes from grasses and rushes. They also used strips of wood. Weavers used two basic techniques—twining and plaiting. In twining, horizontal pieces of hemp cord, known as the weft, were wrapped around the more rigid pieces of bulrushes, called the warp. In the plaited technique, also known as splint basketry, both the weft and the warp were rigid strips of wood such as strips of ash or white oak. The splints were woven alternately over and under to create a checkerboard pattern. Over time, splint baskets became more common and eventually were the only kind of basket made by the Wampanoag. These baskets were made for use during the corn harvest. One splint basket was carried on the back and another larger basket was placed at the edge of the field. Splint baskets were also used as sieves for sifting cornmeal. Small baskets were used for carrying parched cornmeal on journeys, and corn was placed in large baskets in storage pits.

The Wampanoag made dishes and other objects from clay, stone, and minerals. They collected quartz and slate for making tools and weapons. From various outcroppings, they quarried other minerals, such as limonite and hematite, from which they extracted yellow and red pigments. From soft soapstone, they carved bowls and pipes. The Wampanoag traded pottery, wooden bowls, and wampum with other native peoples in exchange for copper to be fashioned into ornaments. From Europeans they obtained metal pots and kettles and learned to cast pewter, brass, and lead into ornaments, buttons, and ammunition.

Clay for making pots was readily available around Plymouth and at Aquinnah, which was later called Gay Head because of the

*T*his *detail of a basket illustrates the fine weaving, delicate colors, and intricate designs favored by the Wampanoag.*

colorful clay found at the cliffs. The Wampanoag shaped these brilliant clays into pots, bowls, and jugs. The objects were then sun-dried instead of fired, because firing in a kiln dulled the colors. Pottery is still one of the most distinctive and striking of Wampanoag handicrafts.

4. Beliefs

The Wampanoag believed in Kiehtan,
a supreme being who created
the earth itself, including
the land and the sea.

THE WAMPANOAG RECOGNIZED A SUPREME BEING AND CREATOR KNOWN AS Kiehtan and many lesser gods. The Wampanoag believed that all of creation—the plants, the animals, and the earth itself—was imbued with spirits. Striving to live in harmony with the woods and the water around them, they did not distinguish between the physical and spiritual aspects of the natural world. People did not believe themselves to be superior to animals. They respected all other living creatures. When deer were hunted and plants harvested, the Wampanoag acknowledged their sacrifice and expressed gratitude to the spirit of the animal or plant.

Like other native peoples, the Wampanoag believed that all of nature, including plants, had spirits.

Manitous—*which could be rocks as well as plants and animals—could either aid or impair the Wampanoag.*

People believed that various spirits could use supernatural powers known as *manitous* to help or hinder them. Animals, plants, or even objects such as rocks could have manitous. An individual would have good fortune if he glimpsed, touched, or dreamed about a manitou that was symbolized by one of these spirits. The Wampanoag strongly believed in the significance of dreams. A bad dream was regarded as a warning or threat from the supernatural, and when the dreamer awakened, he immediately prayed for help. If the dream was particularly ominous, he asked his friends to watch over him. He offered food to them, but fasted himself and remained awake for several days and nights. In a good dream, one's fortune would be improved, especially if a guardian spirit appeared. This guardian spirit could be called upon whenever help was needed.

Rites and Ceremonies

Blending religion and medicine, powwows were responsible for healing the spirit and the body. The term *powwow* refers to a shamanic method of acquiring power. A man—and occasionally a woman—became a powwow through a dream in which he or she was chosen by an animal spirit. (The Algonquian term *powwow* has come to mean a modern Indian festival.) The individual then announced the dream to others in the community and a two-day celebration was held. With the help of their own animal spirits, powwows conducted rituals and treated illnesses and injuries with herbal medicines. They also mediated with the spirit world to help with these cures and to forecast the weather.

Throughout the year, the Wampanoag held ceremonies that included feasting, singing, dancing, and playing games. On many occasions, they gave thanks for an abundant harvest, good health, and peace. At least twice a year, several Wampanoag bands came together for a large gathering. Every spring, they held a celebration at the fish camps. In the fall, they enjoyed a harvest festival in which everyone danced through the night. There were also small private feasts, notably the Nikomo or Nickommo, held in the winter. A family invited a small group of guests to this feast at which the host gave away much of his wealth. During times of hardships—war, drought, famine, and illness—the Wampanoag gathered to call upon the spirits for assistance. They offered prayers until the drought was broken or the other adversity was ended. In all these ceremonies, people danced, sang, and offered gifts to please the spirits.

Today, the Wampanoag hold annual ceremonies to honor the traditions of their ancestors. In the Legends of Moshup Pageant, held every summer at Aquinnah, people dress in buckskin clothing and listen to stories. In the autumn, everyone gathers for a harvest festival known as Cranberry Day, the most important annual event for the Wampanoag living on Martha's Vineyard. Parents and children harvest the tart red cranberries during the morning, then in the afternoon gather around a fire to listen to stories. In the evening, people eat a dinner, followed by singing, dancing, and giving thanks.

Games and Gambling

The Wampanoag enjoyed playing games and gambling. Their most important team sport was called "football" by the English. Posts set about a mile apart on the long sandy beaches served as goals. Players tried to get a ball about the size of a tennis ball over the opponent's goal without using their hands. Men put their weapons aside but still painted themselves as though going to war.

On these beaches, the Wampanoag often gathered for games, including a kind of football in which goalposts were set up on the sand.

The competition was fierce. In the rough play, bones were often broken. The contest might go on for two days before a team scored a goal and the game was over. Betting on the outcome was heavy. When tribes played against each other, the goalposts were hung with a wealth of wagered goods, including wampum. Large crowds of women, children, and old men gathered to watch the game and cheer for their team. Despite the vigorous play, there were few quarrels and after the game everyone gathered for a great feast.

Individuals also challenged each other to contests of strength and skill in archery, running, and swimming. Such contests usually attracted large audiences, especially when members of different tribes competed. Many bets were placed. People were especially interested in marksmanship contests with bows and arrows. English visitors were impressed with the skill and endurance of the swimmers. Similarly Wampanoag runners balanced speed with endurance, running great distances for a full day or more.

The Wampanoag played a gambling game called *hubhub*. In hubhub, five bone dice, painted black on one side and white on the other, were placed in a wooden dish. The dish was struck hard on the ground to make the dice bounce in the air. People bet on what combination of colors would turn up. When hubhub was played between teams from different villages, an arbor of four long poles was built for each team. These poles were draped with wampum that was wagered on the game. Hundreds of people came to watch hubhub contests held between villages.

Men, in particular, loved games and gambling. They avidly competed against each other even when there was no audience. A group of men could become engrossed in a game all day and through the night without pausing to sleep or eat. They called upon the spirits to help them win and sometimes carried a rock crystal charm, thought to be a piece of a thunderbolt, to improve their chances. Men might gamble away all their belongings, even the moccasins on their feet. Despite the intense competition, they usually parted company peacefully.

Storytelling

Stories helped people to understand their history and heritage. Among the favorite stories were those about the supernatural deeds of Moshup. Whenever a fog settles over the coastal waters, the Wampanoag believe that it is Moshup's way of reminding people that he is still there, watching over them. Moshup not only formed the island of Martha's Vineyard, but he also showed people many ways in which they could provide for themselves. Here is a short story about Moshup and how he taught the people how to hunt whales, known as *pottap*:

Moshup and Pottap

Moshup became the first whaler in Aquinnah when he caught whales as they swam near shore. He took the whales to his den and often invited others in the Wampanoag community to join him in a great feast. To cook the pottap, he yanked up trees and built a great fire. Today, trees are scarce on Aquinnah because Moshup used so many to stoke the fires of his feasts.

Moshup taught the Wampanoag to follow schools of blackfish to locate the whales. Many of his children and followers took up whaling, too.

Stories helped to remind the Wampanoag of their origins and how their homeland, including Martha's Vineyard, was formed long ago.

5. Changing World

With the arrival of the Pilgrims and other European colonists, the Wampanoag were forced to adapt to a completely new way of life.

THE WAMPANOAG WERE AMONG THE FIRST NATIVE PEOPLE TO ENCOUNTER the Pilgrims after they landed at Plymouth Rock in 1620. Grand Sachem Massasoit, who ruled over all the Wampanoag, sent a man named Squanto as an envoy and translator to greet the Pilgrims. Several years earlier, Squanto had been kidnapped and taken to Europe where he learned English. When he was taken back to North America, Squanto escaped and returned to the Wampanoag. It is believed that Squanto surprised the Pilgrims by speaking English when he encountered them on the beach.

Massasoit helped the inexperienced newcomers during their first hard winter in the new land and generally tried to live peacefully with them. He agreed to a treaty of friendship with the Pilgrims, mostly out of necessity because many of his people had died in an epidemic just before they had arrived. He also hoped to forge an alliance with the Pilgrims against the Narragansett. The Wampanoag helped the Pilgrims grow crops and to provide for themselves. The Wampanoag also joined the Pilgrims in what has become known as the first Thanksgiving. In turn, the Pilgrims traded European goods, such as iron kettles and metal knives, to the Wampanoag.

As other colonies were founded in New England, the Wampanoag remained peaceful. They even befriended Roger Williams, a prominent theologian who rebelled against many of the Puritan teachings. Accused of heresy, Williams fled Salem and the Massachusetts Bay Colony to establish the colony of Providence Plantations in what is now Rhode Island. During his journey, he got

This nineteenth-century engraving depicts Massasoit being received with honor by the Pilgrims.

caught in a snowstorm and would most likely have perished, if the Wampanoag had not found and sheltered him. Williams met Massasoit when the grand sachem was about thirty years old. Williams later declared that the two men quickly became "great friends." Williams also befriended Canonicus, the elderly leader of the Narragansett, and traveled the woods for days with both of the chiefs.

By the mid-1600s, tensions were mounting between the New England colonists and the native peoples. When Massasoit died in 1661, he was succeeded by his son Wamsutta, also called Alexander. Ordered to report to the English at Plymouth, Wamsutta died on his way home. Some said he had been poisoned. Massasoit's second son then became sachem of the Wampanoag. This sachem, Metacom, came to be known as Philip and sometimes as King Philip. He renewed peace with the English, but relations became strained as colonists further encroached on Wampanoag lands and devastated the forests and game. The English pushed the declining native peoples into smaller communities or forced them into "praying towns," villages established by ministers. The colonists also deceived the Wampanoag, often with the use of alcohol, into giving up their lands. Sickness swept through the villages. In 1671, there were about forty thousand colonists in New England while the native population, which included the Wampanoag, had dwindled to about twenty thousand people. The farm fields and pastures of the colonists spread, driving away game and angering the Wampanoag. By 1675, the Wampanoag had one remaining strip of land, which the colonists also wanted.

"Soon after I became sachem they disarmed all my people," Philip declared. "I am determined not to live until I have no country." Having reached a breaking point, he led his people, who had moved to the area around present-day Bristol, Rhode Island, in an effort to unite all the tribes in southern New England in what came to be known as King Philip's War. The war broke out on June 20, 1675, at the settlement of Swansea and quickly spread across southern New England. The Wampanoag, allied with the Narragansett and other native peoples, hoped to drive the British completely out of their territory. Considered a brilliant military strategist, Philip led Wampanoag and Narragansett warriors in many victories at the beginning of the war and nearly succeeded in destroying the colonies. Hundreds of colonists were slaughtered—nearly half the population of English settlers. However, some warriors began to fight before the campaign had been completely prepared, leading many warriors to refuse to join the alliance. Betrayed by traitors and cut off from supplies, Philip retreated to the cedar swamps of Rhode Island. In August 1676, he was defeated and killed in battle, effectively ending the offensive campaign in southern New England.

Colonial militia then ruthlessly hunted down and killed Wampanoag and other native peoples, including those who had remained neutral or friendly during the war. After a few months of fierce fighting, the English finally prevailed. The heads of Philip and Weetamo, Wamsutta's widow, were displayed as a warning on posts. Most of the natives remaining in the area were either killed or enslaved. Many widows and children were sold as slaves in the West Indies. Philip's son was auctioned off with

*I*n King Philip's War, the Wampanoag and other native allies attacked settlements in hopes of driving colonists from their homeland.

about five hundred other native people. The Wampanoag and Narragansett, in particular, were nearly wiped out.

A handful of survivors managed to escape to the interior—some journeying as far as the Great Lakes region and Canada. Others fled to Cape Cod and nearby islands where they joined Wampanoag communities that had not taken part in the war. Both friendly natives and enemy warriors were forced onto reservations called plantations. For centuries after this conflict, the Wampanoag suffered mistreatment as servants and discrimination in general. At best, they were forgotten and ignored. In some instances, they were not able to survive in a rapidly changing world. The native population on Nantucket Island declined from about 1,500 in 1600 to 358 in 1763, and then to only twenty people in 1792, mainly as a result of disease. The last native person there died in 1855.

The Wampanoag in other areas of New England fared somewhat better. The people living at Mashpee, Cape Cod, were granted fifty square miles of land as a plantation in 1660. They fought to establish and maintain their own self-governed community. Over the years, Wampanoag people from other areas of the Cape came to live in Mashpee and by 1700 the tribe had its own recognized territory. Although many of their traditional beliefs had been suppressed in an attempt to Christianize them, the Wampanoag continued to believe in Moshup.

Throughout the eighteenth century, the Wampanoag at Mashpee had their own independent tribal community. However, Massachusetts, first as a colony and then as a commonwealth, frequently intervened in their affairs. In 1788, the Commonwealth of Massachusetts placed the

Wampanoag under its control. Declaring the settlement to be a plantation, Massachusetts appointed overseers to help in managing the community, and alternately protected Wampanoag lands and defended its own illegal seizures of tribal territory. In 1833, the Wampanoag rebelled against these intrusions on their land. Led by "Blind Joe" Amos, Isaac Coombs, Ezra Attaquin, and William Apes, a Pequot minister, the Mashpee Wampanoag overthrew their Anglo minister, took control of their meetinghouse, and forbid the cutting of trees on their land. Apes and the other leaders were imprisoned but released after order was reestablished. The Massachusetts legislature responded in 1834 by changing the status of Mashpee from "plantation" to a district for native peoples. Mashpee was to be governed as a town, but tribal ownership and control of land was recognized, an arrangement that lasted for twenty-seven years. However, in 1870, the legislature devastated the tribe by dividing most of its land into indi-

When Wampanoag children attended school, they were encouraged to abandon the traditional ways of their parents and ancestors.

vidual parcels. Then, in 1850, the Herring Pond Reservation near Mashpee was allotted. The Mashpee Wampanoag still managed their town government but lost much of their land.

The Mashpee Wampanoag worked as day laborers, domestic servants, farmers, whalers, soldiers, and basket makers. Around 1840, a Wampanoag named Solomon Attaquin established a popular vacation resort that was visited by writer Henry David Thoreau and statesman Daniel Webster. The resort thrived until 1954 when it was destroyed in a fire. Over the years, several small Wampanoag communities died out or merged with others, yet the Wampanoag strived to preserve and continue traditional beliefs and ceremonies.

In 1602 about three thousand Wampanoag lived on Martha's Vineyard. In 1641, Thomas Mayhew purchased Martha's Vineyard, Nantucket, and the Elizabeth Islands from the British for forty pounds. The newcomers brought European diseases for which the Wampanoag had little or no resistance. By 1674 there were around 1,200 Wampanoag living on Martha's Vineyard. The people on the three reservations on the island—Chappaquiddick, Christiantown, and Gay Head—were also forced to adapt to a society that nearly destroyed their traditional way of life. In 1870, the principal Wampanoag community on the island, centered at Aquinnah (Gay Head), was granted town status by the Commonwealth of Massachusetts. By 1900, of the three Wampanoag groups on the island, only the one at Aquinnah remained. Never governed by non-natives, they have been better able to preserve their heritage and assert their contemporary rights than have other Wampanoag groups.

Wampanoag Language

The Wampanoag spoke the Massachusett language, one of five Algonquian languages spoken in southern New England. The other languages were Loup, Narragansett, Mohegan-Pequot-Montauk, and Quiripi-Unquachog. Each of these languages was so similar that speakers of the different languages could usually understand each other. What is known of the Massachusett language comes largely from John Eliot's 1663 translation of the Bible into that language. Today, the language survives in place names, such as Aquinnah, known in English as Gay Head; Hyannis from *Iyanough*, meaning "warrior's place;" and Mashpee, meaning "great pond." The first syllables of the names Massachusetts, meaning "big hill;" Mississippi, meaning "big river;" and Massasoit, meaning "big or great chief," are drawn from the Algonquian *massa*.

Using written historical documents of missionaries and the knowledge of native speakers, the people of Aquinnah and Mashpee are reclaiming their language. Assisted by linguists and language classes, the Language Reclamation Project has established both a short- and a long-term plan to ensure that the Wampanoag language is recovered and kept alive for future generations. Following is a sampling of words from *One of the Keys*, compiled and written by Milton A. Travers in 1975, that offers a sense of the people, places, objects, and values important to the Wampanoag.

Nature

clear water, as in a brook or pool	mashtuxet
cloud	mattauquas
dew	neechipog
earth	ohbee
fair weather	wekineauquat
frost	taquattin
great frost	missittopu
great wind	mishaupen
high tide	keesaqushin
hot weather	kausitteks
ice	capat
light	wequai
lightning	cutshausha
moonlight	wequashim
my land (this is my land)	nittauke nissawanawkamuck
pond	nips
rain	sokenun
storm	mishitashin
sun	nippawus
thunder	neimpauog
tree, or trees	mihtuck-quash
wind	waupi or waban

Places/Travel

to anchor or tie up a boat	kunnosnep
by an island	aquetnet
beyond the water	accomac
cove	aucup
far out to sea	nawwatick
good place to set camp	mattapan
good places for shellfishing	naskeag
meadow	micuckaskeete
names for a sachem's house	chicka, sachimmaacommock
orchard	ahtuck
place in the hills	natick
river	seip
sea	wechekum
to go by water	acawmuck
village, or villages	otan-nash
woods	weta

Objects

acorns	anauchemineash
basket, or baskets	munnote-tash
beads made from the shell of the quahog	wampum
corn	ewachim-neash
buckskin	causkashunck

dugout	mishoon
fishing line	aumanep
girdle of wampum	machequoce
hatchet	chichegin
shells (from shellfish)	anawsuck
soft leather shoes	mocussinass or mockussinchass

Animals

clams	sukkissuog-quahog
dog	anum
ducks	quaquecum-mauog
lobster	ashaunt
oysters	opponenauhock
porpoise	tatackommauog
turkey, or turkeys	neyhome-mauog

People

chief who ruled more than one Wampanoag tribe	sachem
female chief	squaw sachem
friend, or friends	netop-pauog
maiden	keegsquaw
one who makes a feast	awaun-nakommit
one who makes the wampum	natouwompitea
warrior	mecautea
wise men	wauontakick

Spiritual World

devil, one of the evil spirits	hobomoko
god	manitou
fire god	yotaanit
moon god	nanepaushat
soul or spirit	cowwewonck
sun god	keesuckquant

Times

to dry corn	pausinnummin
noontime	paweshaquaw
peace	aquene
planting time	aukeeteaumitch
sunrise	paspisha
time of leisure and storytelling	hawkswawney
truce	awepu

6. New Ways

Some Wampanoag people support themselves by operating charter fishing boats at Aquinnah, on Martha's Vineyard.

TODAY THERE ARE FIVE WAMPANOAG GROUPS IN MASSACHUSETTS, AT Aquinnah (Gay Head), Mashpee, Assonet, Herring Pond, and Nemasket. Each has a written constitution, a chief, and an elected tribal council. There is also a council of chiefs for all the Wampanoag, and the mainland Wampanoag recognize a spiritual leader. Another group, the Pokanoket Tribe of the Wampanoag Nation, is located in Bristol, Rhode Island. Led by descendants of Massasoit, the Pokanoket Tribe is seeking federal recognition and ownership of 267 acres of land in Bristol, Rhode Island. The two largest groups of Wampanoag are concentrated in Mashpee on Cape Cod and at Aquinnah on Martha's Vineyard.

In the 1920s, the Mashpee Wampanoag and other Wampanoag people in Massachusetts began to reclaim their rights and rebuild their identity as a native people—a vigorous effort that continues to the present. In 1928, two individuals, Eben Queppish, who had been a performer in Buffalo Bill Cody's Wild West Show, and Nelson Simon, who had attended the Carlisle Indian Industrial School in Pennsylvania, united the Mashpee, Gay Head, and Herring Pond communities as the Wampanoag Nation. After Queppish died in an automobile accident in 1933, the Mashpee Wampanoag divided into factions. By the 1960s, the town of Mashpee, like the rest of Cape Cod, was experiencing a frenzy of development. New housing and shifting populations changed Mashpee's voting patterns, and the Wampanoag lost control of the town government and the marine resources on which many people depended for their livelihood. By 1974, nonnatives had come to control the Mashpee

*E*ben Queppish, along with Nelson Simon, worked hard to unite the Mashpee, Gay Head, and Herring Pond Wampanoag.

town government. The tribe fought these changes by incorporating and filing a lawsuit under the Trade and Intercourse Act to recover lands taken away in 1870. The case went to federal court, but in 1978 a jury determined that the Mashpee was not a tribe and therefore not entitled to its land claim.

Under Grand Sachem Ellsworth Oakley, or Drifting Goose, the Mashpee Wampanoag were able to add the Assonet and Nemasket groups and reorganize in 1975. However, the tribe was denied federal recognition in 1979. Since then leaders have appealed the ruling. Despite the court decision, the Mashpee Wampanoag are

*U*ntil 1968, Wampanoag children attended Gay Head School, which was built in 1827 and enlarged in 1857. The building now houses the town library.

*T*he Wampanoag community at Aquinnah now manages tribal lands, which include docks for fishing boats.

continuing their struggle for recognition and ownership of a land base. They are governed by the thirteen members of the Mashpee Wampanoag Indian Tribal Council. The tribe also has two honored leaders, a chief and shaman whose positions were reestablished during the cultural revival of the 1920s. Today, about 500 of the 1,000 Mashpee Wampanoag live in the town of Mashpee.

In 1987, the Wampanoag at Gay Head (Aquinnah) were federally recognized as a tribe. Today about 700 people trace their heritage to the Wampanoag on Martha's Vineyard, about 250 of which live on the island. The Gay Head Wampanoag owns in trust several parcels of land on Martha's Vineyard totaling about 150 acres. The tribe is now struggling to regain sovereignty over all of Aquinnah. The Wampanoag have managed to achieve a measure of self-government in their daily lives, notably in regard to managing health services, offering scholarship programs, and protecting the local environment. They are governed by a tribal council having a chairperson and twelve members. Elected by the Aquinnah Wampanoag, the tribal council represents the people in all matters relating to the tribe. Tribal facilities include a community building that houses the tribal offices and space for the bi-monthly council meetings and general membership meetings. In recent years, the Gay Head Wampanoag have established vigorous cultural, educational, and social service programs. The tribe is constructing additional housing, and many members hope to return and again make their home on Martha's Vineyard.

Wherever they live, the Wampanoag are striving to preserve many elements of their culture. They like to believe that Moshup, who created Martha's Vineyard and its neighboring islands, still guides their destiny. Every year, the Gay Head Wampanoag hold important ceremonies, notably the Moshup Pageant in August and Cranberry Day in October. Blending stories, music, and dramatic performances, the Moshup Pageant recalls and honors Moshup's life. Although Cranberry Day once lasted three or four

*T*he Gay Head Wampanoag strengthen the bonds of community and tradition through singing and dancing on Cranberry Day.

Wampanoag society is still based on close-knit families, which like to get together for Cranberry Day and other celebrations.

days, this day-long festival is still more significant and meaningful to the Wampanoag than any other holiday.

The Mashpee Wampanoag host a powwow on the Fourth of July Indian Day and the Assonet Wampanoag have an annual Strawberry Festival. Although the Wampanoag do not have their own schools, they are working to have native history and culture included in school curricula. Efforts have been made to revive customs such as gathering plants for food and medicine and the traditional arts and crafts. The Wampanoag hope to pass on their deeply-held beliefs and traditions to their children and grandchildren.

More about

the Wampanoag

Timeline

1602 Bartholomew Gosnold explores Vineyard Sound, the Elizabeth Islands, and Buzzards Bay. An unsuccessful attempt is made to establish a trading post on Cuttyhunk Island in Wampanoag territory.

1603 Martin Pring explores lower Cape Cod. He trades with the native people but also antagonizes them with large dogs called mastiffs.

1605–1606 Samuel de Champlain leads French expeditions as far south as Cape Cod to explore and trade with the native people.

1616–1619 Major epidemic of European diseases reaches Wampanoag villages and devastates the population.

1620 The Wampanoag meet the Pilgrims, who have just arrived in New England.

1621 Grand Sachem Massasoit signs the Treaty of Amity with the Pilgrims.

1628 Massachusetts Bay Colony is established with a large number of settlers.

1631 Smallpox epidemic sweeps through Massachusetts Bay area.

1633 Another smallpox epidemic spreads from New England into southern Ontario.

1636 Roger Williams is expelled from the Massachusetts Bay Colony and flees to what is now Providence, Rhode Island, in territory fought over by the Wampanoag and Narragansett.

1639 Massasoit and his son Metacom (Philip) reaffirm their agreement with Plymouth Colony not to cause any unjust war or sell any land without consent of the colony.

1650 John Eliot founds the first "praying Indian" mission at Natick under the authority of the Massachusetts Bay Colony.

1661 Massasoit dies.

1663 John Eliot publishes the Bible in the Massachusett language.

1671 After being accused of conspiracy, Philip is forced to submit to colonial authority.

1675–1676 King Philip's War leads to the slaughter and enslavement of most Wampanoag people.

1676 Philip is killed in an ambush at Montaup.

1833–1834 Mashpee Revolt leads to limited self-government for the Wampanoag living at Mashpee.

1928 Three Wampanoag groups in Massachusetts unify as the Wampanoag Nation.

1987 Gay Head Wampanoag receive federal recognition.

Notable People

Alexander (Wamsutta) (died 1662), leader, was given his English name, after Alexander of ancient Macedonia, on his own request by the court of Plymouth. The son of Massasoit and brother of Philip, he was first in succession as grand sachem when his father died in 1661. Like his father, he sought to continue peaceful relations with the colonists. However, Plymouth leaders, suspecting a Wampanoag and Narragansett conspiracy, summoned Alexander to a hearing. He refused to come and a group of ten colonists, led by Josiah Winslow, went in search of Alexander. They found him feasting in a hunting lodge with his men near present-day Halifax, Massachusetts. Accompanied by his warriors and some of the women, including his wife Weetamo, Alexander was forced to come to Plymouth for a trial. On the way, he became ill with a high fever and the Wampanoag were allowed to take him home. Alexander died on the return journey. Weetamo suspected that her husband had been poisoned by the colonists. The death of Alexander was followed by heightened tensions between the Wampanoag and the colonists.

Annawan (Annawon, Anawon) (died 1676), war leader, distinguished himself under Massasoit as *missinnege* of the *pnieses*, or head of the war leaders. He also served as Philip's principal counselor and strategist. When Philip was killed in August 1676, Annawan took command of the Wampanoag warriors and attacked the colonial settlements of Swansea and Plymouth. Moving camp every night, he eluded Benjamin Church and his men until an informer helped the colonists locate Annawan in a swamp along the Rehoboth River on August 26, 1676. At the site now known as Annawan's Rock, the colonists were able to seize most of the warriors' weapons and convince Annawan to surrender. He turned over his tribe's medicine bundle, a deerskin wrapped around a large wampum belt detailing the Wampanoag's history, a small wampum belt representing the confederacy, two powder horns, and a red blanket that had belonged to Philip. The relinquishment of these objects symbolized the end of the war. The prisoners were taken to Plymouth for a trial. Colonial authorities in Plymouth ordered Annawan to be executed. Church, who had come to respect the great leader, argued that Annawan should be spared. However, while Church was away, an angry mob seized Annawan and beheaded him. With the death of the war leader, the Wampanoag Confederacy ended.

Awashonks (active 1670s), sachem, became the leader of the Sakonnet tribe, in the area of present-day Little Compton, Rhode Island, after her husband died. Her tribe was a member of the Wampanoag Confederacy, and during King Philip's War of 1675–1676, she permitted some of her warriors to take part in the revolt. After meeting with Benjamin Church, she switched sides and supported the colonists. Some of her warriors, including her son Peter Awashonks, then fought against the Wampanoag who had been their allies.

Corbitant (Conbitant, Caunbitant) (active 1620s), sachem, possibly the father of Weetamo, was the leader of the Pocasset and Mattapoisett bands, which lived in the area of present-day Tiverton, Rhode Island, and Fall River, Massachusetts. When Grand Sachem Massasoit signed the Treaty of Amity at Plymouth on September 13, 1621, Corbitant argued for resistance against the Europeans, whom he considered to be invaders. He tried to establish a military alliance with the Narragansett and other tribes to drive the colonists back into the sea. He also plotted against Squanto and Hobomok, seizing the two friends of the colonists when colonial leader Miles Standish was away. Hobomok managed to escape and lead Standish and his men to the scene of the attack. After a show of force by the soldiers under Standish, Corbitant accepted a treaty with the colonists.

Hobomok (Hobomoko, Hobbamock) (active 1620–1642), one of Massasoit's councilors, was sent as a special envoy to assist the Pilgrims after they landed at Plymouth in 1620. Along with Squanto, he provided food and showed the colonists how to live in the wilderness, helping them to survive their first hard winter in North America. He served as a liaison between Massasoit and the colonists and as a military advisor to Miles Standish. In August 1621, Hobomok and Squanto were attacked by warriors under Corbitant but managed to escape and inform Standish, who quelled the insurrection. Hobomok converted to Christianity and lived among the colonists at Plymouth until his death in 1642.

Iyanough (Iyannos, Yannis, Jannos) (died 1623), tribal leader, headed the Mattakeeset band, which lived on Cape Cod near present-day Barnstable and Hyannis Port, Massachusetts. A sub-sachem under Grand Sachem Massasoit, he helped the Pilgrims during their first years at Plymouth Colony. With Aspinet of the Nauset, he rescued a boy named John Billington who had become lost in the spring of 1621 and returned him to his parents. In the spring of 1623, Massasoit warned the colonists that Iyanough and Aspinet and leaders of the Massachusett and Narragansett were plotting against them. Miles Standish responded by attacking the hostile warriors and driving them into the swamps. While in hiding, both Iyanough and Aspinet died, apparently from diseases they had caught from the colonists.

Massasoit (Woosamequin, Wasamegin, Osamekin, Yellow Feather) (1580–1661), grand sachem of the Wampanoag in the 1600s, wielded considerable influence over several native groups from Narragansett Bay to Cape Cod. He encouraged peaceful relations with the English colonists, and often negotiated agreements with the settlers. As early as 1621, with the help of Squanto, who spoke English, Massasoit established friendly trading relationships with the Pilgrims at Plymouth Colony. He traded food in exchange for tools, firearms, and other European goods.

Massasoit offered advice on farming and hunting and gave land to the colonists. He also recommended ways that the Puritan colonists could defend themselves against other tribes. In 1623, he warned them of an impending attack by hostile warriors. Massasoit's alliance with the colonists triggered hostility from those tribes that opposed the English colonists, and the Wampanoag often had to fight these tribes.

The great leader became friends with Roger Williams, a prominent theologian and leader. It is believed that Massasoit influenced Williams' views about the rights of Native Americans. When Williams was accused of heresy and threatened with imprisonment by the Massachusetts colonial government, he fled to Massasoit's home for protection. Despite the efforts of Williams to keep peace, Massasoit came to resent the incessant demands of the English colonists for more land. However, it was Massasoit's son, Philip, who actually went to war with the colonists in 1675.

Although the actual events have been obscured by myths, it is recorded that Massasoit took part in the first Thanksgiving. In 1621, he and several followers came to Plymouth where they feasted for several days with the Pilgrims. Massasoit and his people supplied five deer for this historic meal.

Peters, John (1930–1997), spiritual leader, was born in Hyannis, but grew up in the nearby town of Mashpee on Cape Cod. A descendant of the Wampanoag people who first met the Pilgrims, he grew up in a community that strongly maintained traditional beliefs and customs. His family had long been involved in tribal affairs and local politics, his father serving as a Mashpee selectman for twenty-five years. As a child, Peters was apprenticed to Billy James, a Mashpee shaman, and eventually became the spiritual leader for a half dozen Wampanoag groups. In this position, he presided over naming ceremonies, funerals, and other tribal gatherings.

Actively involved in politics, he frequently lobbied on behalf of his people at the Massachusetts State House. He participated in conferences across the nation and lobbied with other Native American leaders on many common interests, including the American Indian Religious Freedom Act of 1978 and the Indian Child Welfare Act of 1978. He also worked on legislation, first in Massachusetts and then in the U.S. Congress, to require the return of skeletal remains to their tribes. Under the federal law, known as the Native American Graves Protection and Repatriation Act, museums and federal agencies must offer to return Native American remains and funerary objects held in their collections.

Philip (King Philip, Metacom, Metacomet) (about 1639–1676), grand sachem, and his brother Wamsutta requested English names from the colonial court and were given the ancient Greek names of Philip and Alexander. He became known as King Philip during the conflict that was named after him. His father Massasoit advocated peaceful relations with the colonists. However, over the years, tension mounted as colonists encroached on native lands. After Massasoit's death in late 1661, Alexander became grand sachem, but he died the next year, shortly after being summoned to appear before colonial authorities. His widow, Weetamo, who ruled as sachem over the Wampanoag Pocasset band, suspected that the colonists had poisoned him. Philip probably also suspected foul play when he became grand sachem in 1662 while in his early twenties.

Philip, whose main village was situated at Mount Hope on the west shore of Mount Hope Bay near present-day Bristol, Rhode Island, continued friendly relations with the colonists. He even sold large tracts of land to the newcomers into the late 1670s. However, during this time, he was also organizing other tribes and planning an uprising. Hearing rumors of the revolt, colonial officials ordered the Wampanoag to surrender their guns and sign two treaties. Philip agreed to these conditions because he needed more time. Hostilities in King Philip's War began in 1675, when a confederacy of Massachusett, Mohegan, Niantic, and Wampanoag tribes, with support from the Nauset and Sakonnet, attacked the colonists. Led by Benjamin Church, the colonists retaliated, destroying the native villages.

Battles continued through the summer and early winter. By the spring of 1676, the rebellion had been crushed and the colonial soldiers began hunting down small defiant bands. In May, Philip's wife Wootonekanuske and his young son were captured. Philip was hiding in Bridgewater Swamp, but Church located him and attacked at dawn on August 12, 1676. In the ensuing battle, Philip was shot and killed.

Squanto (Tisquantum) (about 1580–1622), ally of the Pilgrims, was a member of the Patuxet band which lived on Cape Cod. It is believed that Squanto was kidnapped in 1614 and taken to Spain with other native people and sold into slavery by an English trader named Captain Thomas Hunt. He may have been ransomed by a sympathetic Englishman and taken to England. In 1618 or 1619, he returned to his homeland with Captain Thomas Dermer. He was the only one of the Patuxet captives who had survived an epidemic, most likely of smallpox, which had broken out in 1616 and raged for three years.

Somoset, an Abenaki living with the Wampanoag, introduced Squanto to Massasoit and the Pilgrims in March 1621. The grand sachem employed Squanto as an envoy and interpreter to the Pilgrims and helped them to survive their early years at Plymouth Colony. Along with Massasoit, Squanto helped to bring about the first Thanksgiving feast in the fall of 1621. He was also involved in hostilities between the Pilgrims and native peoples, notably when Corbitant, who was plotting against the colonists, tried to kidnap him. Squanto was able to escape and warn the colonists of the plot against them.

In the autumn of 1622, Squanto agreed to accompany the Pilgrims as guide and interpreter on a trading mission for food with the Narragansett. Heavy seas forced their ship *Swan* to seek shelter in Chatham Harbor along Cape Cod. Squanto arranged for trade with the local people there. He contracted a fever, probably smallpox, and died at Chatham Harbor.

Squanto

Weetamo (Wetamoo) (1638–1676), sachem, was born near what is now Tiverton, Rhode Island, and became one of the leaders in King Philip's War. After the death of her first husband, she married Alexander (Wamsutta), who succeeded Massasoit as grand sachem. When Alexander died in 1662, probably from an illness, Weetamo suspected that he had been poisoned. As sachem of the Pocasset band in King Philip's War of 1675–1676, she led attacks on the English colonists. During the Great Swamp Fight of December 1675 in southern Rhode Island, she helped her warriors elude capture. On August 6, 1676, English forces made a surprise attack on her camp in Massachusetts, and she fled down the Taunton River by canoe. The soldiers fired on her, sinking the canoe, and she drowned in the swift current. Her body was later found floating in the Taunton River. The colonists chopped off her head and stuck it on a pole as a gruesome warning to other hostile warriors. Many Native Americans now revere Weetamo as a clever and courageous leader.

Glossary

Algonquian   The most widespread group, or family, of languages spoken in North America. Many Native American tribes speak Algonquian languages, including the Abenaki, Arapaho, Blackfoot, Cheyenne, Delaware, Fox, and Shawnee.

Aquinnah   The Wampanoag name for Gay Head, a part of Martha's Vineyard.

breechcloth   A cloth or skin worn between the legs and around the hips; also breechclout.

buckskin   Deer hide softened by a tanning or curing process.

clan   Members of a large family group who trace their descent from a common ancestor.

Hyannis   A Cape Cod town named for Iyanough, a Wampanoag chief of the 1600s.

Kiehtan   The creator and supreme being believed by the Wampanoag to hold the power of life and death.

King Philip's War   A major effort led by Metacom in 1675 and 1676 "to push the English back into the sea," as the Wampanoag faced devastation and loss of land.

Mashpee   Major Wampanoag community, meaning "big pond" or "big water." Mashpee Pond is the largest body of freshwater on Cape Cod.

Massachusetts   Homeland of the Wampanoag people, meaning "big hill."

Moshup   Heroic giant who created Martha's Vineyard and Cape Cod and who cared for the Wampanoag in ancient times. Also *Maushop*.

Narragansett   Native American people who lived to the west of the Wampanoag.

Noepe   Wampanoag name for the island of Martha's Vineyard.

Pequot   Native American people who lived to the east of the Wampanoag.

Pilgrims   Small group of English immigrants who came to North America seeking religious and political freedom.

pnieses   Honored men, advisors, and bodyguards to a sachem, who also served as war leaders.

Pokanoket   Name that neighbors and early English travelers used to describe the Wampanoag.

powwow   Wampanoag religious leader and healer responsible for rituals and ceremonies. Also a social gathering where Native Americans come together for dancing and sharing native crafts and food.

quahog   Derived from the Wampanoag word paqah, a bivalve mollusk having a purple color along the inside edge of its shell.

sachem   Traditional tribal leader, or chief, responsible for the governance and general welfare of his people.

Wampanoag   Meaning "People of the East" or "People of the Dawn," Native American people who live in southeastern Massachusetts and Rhode Island.

wampum   Valuable beads made of white or purple quahog shells.

weeto   A dome-shaped house covered with bark or mats. Also spelled *wetu*.

Further Information

Readings

The following books were consulted in the research and writing of *The Wampanoag*. The stories "Moshup Creates the Island Noepe" and "Moshup and Pottap" were adapted from a wonderful tale told by tribal elder Helen Manning with Jo-Ann Eccher.

Bragdon, Kathleen J. *Native People of Southern New England, 1500–1659.* Norman: University of Oklahoma Press, 1996.

Bourne, Russell. *The Red King's Rebellion: Racial Politics in New England, 1675–1678.* New York: Oxford University Press, 1991.

Calloway, Colin G., ed. *After King Philip's War: Presence and Persistence in Indian New England.* Hanover, NH: University Press of New England, 1997.

Campisi, Jack. *The Mashpee Indians: Tribe on Trial.* Syracuse, NY: Syracuse University Press, 1991.

Carroll, Patrick, ed. *The Wampanoags and the First Thanksgiving: Teacher Handbook.* Chicago: Everyday Learning, 1997.

Cronon, William. *Changes in the Land: Indians, Colonists, and the Ecology of New England.* New York: Hill and Wang, 1983.

Eliot, John. *John Eliot's Indian Dialogues: A Study in Cultural Interaction.* Edited by Henry W. Bowden and James P. Ronda. Westport, CT: Greenwood Press, 1980.

The Encyclopedia of North American Indians. New York: Marshall Cavendish, 1997.

Hoxie, Frederick E. *Encyclopedia of North American Indians.* Boston: Houghton Mifflin, 1996.

Johansen, Bruce E., and Donald A. Grinde Jr. *The Encyclopedia of Native American Biography*. New York: Henry Holt, 1997.

Langer, Howard J., ed. *American Indian Quotations*. Westport, CT: Greenwood Press, 1996.

Malinowski, Sharon. *Notable Native Americans*. Detroit: Gale Research, 1995.

Malinowski, Sharon, and Anna Sheets. *The Gale Encyclopedia of Native American Tribes*. Detroit: Gale Research, 1998.

Manning, Helen, with Jo-Ann Eccher. *Moshup's Footsteps: The Wampanoag Nation, Gay Head/Aquinnah; the People of First Light*. Aquinnah, MA: Blue Cloud Across the Moon Publishing, 2001.

Marten, Catherine. *The Wampanoags in the Seventeenth Century: An Ethnohistorical Survey*. Plymouth, MA: Plimoth Plantation, 1970.

Mills, Earl, and Betty Breen. *Cape Cod Wampanoag Cookbook: Wampanoag Indian Recipes, Images & Lore*. Santa Fe, NM: Clear Light Publishers, 2001.

Mills, Earl and Alicja Mann. *Son of Mashpee: Reflections of Chief Flying Eagle, a Wampanoag*. North Falmouth, MA: Word Studio, 1996.

Moondancer and Strong Woman. *Wampanoag Cultural History: Voices from Past and Present*. Newport, RI: Aquidneck Indian Council, Inc., 1999.

Mwalim. *A Mixed Medicine Bag: 7 Original Folk-Tales from a Black-Wampanoag Culture*. Mashpee, MA: Talking Drum Press, 1998.

Peirce, Ebenezer Weaver. *Indian History, Biography, and Genealogy Pertaining to the Good Sachem Massasoit of the Wampanoag Tribe, and His Descendants: With an Appendix*. Boston, MA: New England Historic Genealogical Society, 1998.

Pritzker, Barry M. *Native Americans: an Encyclopedia of History, Culture, and Peoples*. Santa Barbara, CA: ABC-CLIO, 1998.

Sturtevant, William C., general ed. *Handbook of North American Indians*. Volume 15. *Northeast*, edited by Bruce G. Trigger. Washington, DC: Smithsonian Institution, 1978.

Travers, Milton A. *One of the Keys, 1676–1776–1976*. Dartmouth, MA: Published for the Nation by the Dartmouth Massachusetts Bicentennial Commission, 1975.

Vaughan, Alden T. *New England Frontier: Puritans and Indians, 1620–1675*. Third edition. Norman: University of Oklahoma Press, 1995.

Children's Books

Averill, Esther Holden. *King Philip, the Indian Chief*. Hamden, CT: Linnet Books, 1993.

Bruchac, Joseph. *Squanto's Journey: The Story of the First Thanksgiving*. San Diego: Silver Whistle, 2000.

DeRubertis, Barbara. *Thanksgiving Day: Let's Meet the Wampanoags and the Pilgrims*. New York: Kane, 1992.

Doherty, Katherine M. and Craig A. Doherty. *The Wampanoag*. New York: Franklin Watts, 1995.

Dubowski, Cathy East. *The Story of Squanto: First Friend to the Pilgrims*. Milwaukee: Gareth Stevens Publishing, 1997.

Fradin, Dennis B. *King Philip: Indian Leader*. Hillside, NJ: Enslow Publishers, 1990.

Grace, Catherine O'Neill and Margaret M. Bruhac with Plimoth Plantation. *1621: A New Look at Thanksgiving*. Washington, DC: National Geographic Society, 2001.

Greene, Jacqueline Dembar. *Powwow: A Good Day to Dance*. New York: Franklin Watts, 1998.

Hennessy, B. G. *One Little, Two Little, Three Little Pilgrims*. New York: Viking, 1999.

Kessel, Joyce K. *Squanto and the First Thanksgiving*. Minneapolis: Carolrhoda Books, 1983.

Lund, Bill. *The Wampanoag Indians*. Mankato, MN: Bridgestone Books, 1998.

Medicine Story. *The Children of the Morning Light: Wampanoag Tales*. New York: Macmillan, 1994.

Metaxas, Eric. *Squanto and the First Thanksgiving*. New York: Rabbit Ears Books, 1996.

Metaxas, Eric. *Squanto and the Miracle of Thanksgiving*. Nashville: Tommy Nelson, 1999.

Peters, Russell M. *Clambake—a Wampanoag Tradition*. Minneapolis: Lerner Publications, 1992.

Raphael, Elaine and Don Bolognese. *The Story of the First Thanksgiving*. New York: Scholastic, 1991.

Roman, Joseph. *King Philip, Wampanoag Rebel*. New York: Chelsea House Publishers, 1992.

Sewall, Marcia. *People of the Breaking Day*. New York: Atheneum, 1990.

Sewall, Marcia. *Thunder from the Clear Sky*. New York, NY: Atheneum Books for Young Readers, 1995.

Waters, Kate. *Giving Thanks: The 1621 Harvest Feast*. New York: Scholastic Press, 2001.

Waters, Kate. *Tapenum's Day: A Wampanoag Indian Boy in Pilgrim Times*. New York: Scholastic, 1996.

Weinstein-Farson, Laurie. *The Wampanoag*. New York: Chelsea House, 1989.

Whitehurst, Susan. *The First Thanksgiving*. PowerKids Press: New York, 2002.

Organizations

Mashpee Wampanoag Tribal Council
P. O. Box 1048
Mashpee, MA 02649
Phone: (508) 477-0208
Fax: (508) 477-1218

Plimoth Plantation
P. O. Box 1620
Plymouth, MA 02362
Phone: (508) 746-1622
Fax: (508) 746-4978

Wampanoag Tribe of Gay Head (Aquinnah)
20 Black Brook Road
Aquinnah, MA 02535-1546
Phone: (508) 645-9265
Fax: (508) 645-3790

Web Sites

Ethnic Groups of New Bedford: Wampanoag
http://www.newbedford.com/ntvamerican.html

Life as a Wampanoag
http://teacher.scholastic.com/thanksgiving/plimoth/wampan1.htm

Northeast Tribes: Wampanoag
http://www.newigwam.com/hwampanoag.html

Plimoth Plantation
http://www.plimoth.org/

Pokanoket Wampanoag Official Homepage
http://www.geocities.com/pokanoket_tribe/

Seaconke Wampanoag Tribe
http://www.inphone.com/seahome.html

Wampanoag
http://pilgrims.net/native_americans/

Wampanoag History
http://www.tolatsga.org/wampa.html

The Wampanoag Indians: A Thanksgiving Lesson
http://www.teachervision.com/lesson-plans/lesson-3358.html

The Wampanoag: People of the First Light
http://www.bostonkids.org/teachers/TC/

The Wampanoag—People of the Dawn
http://www.plimoth.org/Library/library.htm#wamp

Wampanoag Tribe
http://www.vineyard.net/org/mvcc/wpinfo.html

Wampanoag Tribe of Gay Head (Aquinnah)
http://www.wampanoagtribe.net/

Index

Page numbers in **boldface** are illustrations.

women, 14, 19, 29, 33, 36, **37**, **40**, 41, 44,
   47, 48, 49, 50–51, 53, 54, 68, 88
   See also Awashonks; Weetamo
Woosamequin. *See* Massasoit

Yellow Feather. *See* Massasoit

Raymond Bial

HAS PUBLISHED MORE THAN THIRTY CRITICALLY ACCLAIMED BOOKS OF PHO-tographs for children and adults. His photo-essays for children include *Corn Belt Harvest, Amish Home, Frontier Home, Shaker Home, The Underground Railroad, Portrait of a Farm Family, With Needle and Thread: A Book About Quilts, Mist Over the Mountains: Appalachia and Its People, Cajun Home,* and *Where Lincoln Walked.*

He is currently immersed in writing *Lifeways,* a series of books about Native Americans. As with his other work, Bial's deep feeling for his subjects is evident in both the text and illustrations. He travels to tribal cultural centers, photographing homes, artifacts, and surroundings and learning firsthand about the national lifeways of these peoples.

A full-time library director at a small college in Champaign, Illinois, he lives with his wife and three children in nearby Urbana.